T0197092

WORKBOOK

Identifying Your Kingdom
Assignment in the Earth

TYRONE JOHNSON

authorHOUSE®

AuthorHouse™
1663 Liberty Drive
Bloomington, IN 47403
www.authorhouse.com
Phone: 1 (800) 839-8640

Published by AuthorHouse 02/02/2018

ISBN: 978-1-5462-2576-8 (sc)
ISBN: 978-1-5462-2577-5 (hc)
ISBN: 978-1-5462-2575-1 (e)

CONTENTS

FROM THE AUTHOR

Being a pastor for twenty years, I have seen people struggle as they attempt to walk in the will of God. We can be bombarded with unwise council and other peoples' opinions. Sometimes, things work for other people but don't work for us. Trying to make sense out of these things can be a recipe for confusion and discouragement. This workbook is designed to help you identify your kingdom assignment, which is your purpose in the earth, it is written on the premise that when God created you, He placed His purpose for you in your heart. This workbook is a tool to help you to draw out of your heart what God has already placed there. This workbook has several exercises that you must complete so that you will benefit from this workbook. You will be required to go back to previous exercises in order to complete the current exercise, this book has numbered tabs which allows you to find previous exercises quickly, this workbook will only help those who are

serious about walking in their kingdom assignment. If you are prayerful as you complete the exercises in this workbook, the Holy Spirit will lead you in the right direction. Know that I will be praying for you, and God bless you

Pastor Tyrone Johnson

INTRODUCTION

I believe that we are all born curious and searching for our purpose. The problem is, how will we know when we find it? The Live on Purpose Institute polled several groups of people in difference professions and concluded that out of over seven billion people on the earth, less than 5 percent know their purpose with crystal clarity. Out of that 5 percent, less than 2 percent are actually living out their purpose.

Before I accepted Christ into my life, I knew that something was missing in my life, I just didn't know what it was. I never gave it much thought. I just kept on having "fun." But even when doing "fun" things, there was a sense of lack, an emptiness that I felt. In October of 1996, I gave my life to Christ and that gave me some satisfaction, but something was still missing, so the search continued. My search after accepting Christ was

very different than my search before accepting Him. This was a search for my purpose in the earth. I can remember it like it was yesterday. I was in love with God and I wanted to please Him, but I didn't know how. Being a new believer in Christ is like starting a new job. The first few days you feel lost, and you are not sure what you are supposed to be doing or if you are doing things right. You may have someone working beside you, but they are usually a stranger and you are not sure you can trust them or if they even know what they are talking about themselves. So, you hang loose and hope for the best. It is sad to say but that is how most of us begin our walk with the Lord. And some people are still hanging loose and hoping for the best years after they accept Christ.

When you first accepted Christ, there is a sense of excitement and urgency. You know that you should be doing something but you don't know what it is. Your prayer basically consists of "Lord, what should I do?" or "Show me, Lord, show me." If you experienced this when you accepted Christ into your life

or you are still experiencing it years later, don't panic. You are not alone.

It may surprise you to learn that the average Christian who has been living for Christ for ten to twenty years still doesn't know why God created them or what their purpose in the earth is. I have read a lot of books on purpose and have learned that my intuition was right all along—I was created for a purpose, and God has a plan for my life. But knowing that God has a plan for my life and knowing what it is are two very different things. None of the books that I have read told me what my purpose was or showed me how to identify my God-given purpose. A seasoned Christian might say to me, "Ask God," but telling a new believer to ask God is a loaded request. After all, how many times have you thought God had spoken to you and found out later He didn't? Or maybe someone told you, "God told me to tell you…" and later you found out that God had never said anything to them.

In identifying your purpose in the earth, you can't afford to misinterpret what the Holy Spirit says to you. You don't

want to spend twenty years doing something and then find out you were doing the wrong thing. We know that as believers our common purpose is to be like Jesus, which in itself is a great challenge, but what part does each individual believer personally play in helping to bring God's kingdom to earth? What role or position are you supposed to play in the kingdom? What should you be doing now? These are all great questions. This workbook will help you find the answer to these questions regarding your role in the kingdom.

Five things you must settle before beginning this workbook

1) God had a purpose in mind when He created me

2) My purpose is greater than I am

3) God placed my purpose in me

4) God wants me to know and fulfill my purpose

5) Only I can forfeit my purpose

The above five statements you must settle in your heart, or the enemy will talk you out of your God-given destiny every time. Satan would like nothing better than to see you leave this earth with your work undone. As children of God, our greatest fear should not be death, but death with unfinished work.

Chapter I

What Am I Here for?

God doesn't make mistakes

"God doesn't make mistakes" is a statement that we usually hear as a source of comfort when someone dies. I think a more beneficial statement would be about the person that is left alive: God didn't make a mistake when He let you live today or when He woke you up this morning, so what are you going to do with it? You and I are not a mistake. God knew exactly what He was doing when He created us, and He created each one of us with a specific purpose in mind.

God doesn't make mistakes, and He doesn't do things just to be doing them. You don't need anyone else to tell you that there is more to life than what you have been experiencing.

You already know that. You just need to be pointed in the right direction. We can only get our true purpose from God because He is the one who created us, and He certainly knows why.

If you are like most Christians, you may feel that God is playing hide-and-go-seek with your earthly purpose and that you are losing big time. But could it be that you are looking in all the wrong places? A general rule of thumb as you seek your purpose is that it will always be the solution to a problem. Some people may find that their purpose is the solution to a problem that really gets them upset. One thing that gets me upset is when I hear people using the Word of God to manipulate others. Because of that, I have become a student of the Word, and I try to simplify the Word in my writing.

1 John 3:8 gives us a problem that we all had. God sent His son Jesus to be the solution to man's problem, thus this was His purpose.

1 John 3:8 *He that committeth sin is of the devil; for the devil sinneth from the beginning. For this purpose the Son of God was manifested, that he might destroy the works of the devil.*

1 John 3:8 sums up Jesus' purpose in one sentence: to destroy the works of the devil. Man had a problem, which was sin, and Jesus came with the solution. Since Jesus knew why He was physically on the earth,

> *What if*
>
> *What if I identify my purpose and I don't like what it is?*
>
> *Rom. 12:1-2*

He knew what He was supposed to be doing on the earth, and He knew what He was *not* supposed to be doing on the earth. Everything that Jesus did was related to His purpose, which was to destroy the works of the devil.

Knowing our purpose makes all the difference in the world. It lets us know what to allow in our lives, but more importantly, it lets us know what *not* to allow in our lives. Knowing your purpose allows you to make purpose-driven decisions. It keeps you from wasting time doing the wrong things. Knowing your purpose also lets you know who your friends should be, what subjects to study in school, what job to accept, whom to marry, where to live, and what church to attend. Your purpose will always be the answer to a problem, so if the problem was on the earth before you were born, your purpose was too. If you want to be successful in life, find a problem and then figure out how to solve it. If you have a problem with something, you best believe you are not the only one on earth with the problem, and people will pay big money to have their problems solved.

Prayer: *Lord reveal to me problems that you would have me to solve or to help solve. Through the Holy Spirit, allow me to see problem areas that I can get involved in.................................... in Jesus' name, amen.*

Exercise: List three common problems you have noticed that you or others have.

1. _____

_____

_____

2. _____

_____

_____

3. _____

_____

_____

Your purpose is always ahead of you

This may be a hard pill to swallow, but your purpose is greater than you are because your purpose is meant to benefit many people, not just you. Also note that your purpose will always be ahead of you. When you begin to search for your purpose, the first place you should look is your future. You will never find your purpose in your past, although your past may be helpful in pointing you in the right direction. We must understand that God always complete things before He begins them, which means that by the time you get ahold of it, God has already competed it. That is why your God-given purpose will always stay ahead of you. Note:

Eph. 1:11 In whom also we have obtained an inheritance, being predestinated according to the purpose of him who worketh all things after the counsel of his own will

Notice how God has fixed life for you to win. With God, His *will* and His purpose are the same and He has predestined both of them.

To predestine means *"to decree, determine, appoint, or settle beforehand."* What God is saying is that His will and purpose for your life has already been settled beforehand, and He has left it as an inheritance for you. All you have to do is claim your inheritance and walk it out, because God has already completed it.

Eph. 1:12 That we should be to the praise of his glory, who first trusted in Christ.

Just as God received glory when Christ fulfilled his purpose, God also receives glory when you fulfill your purpose. Imagine if you were to build a machine and it worked just as you planned it to. Wouldn't that give you a sense of satisfaction? Well your God feels the same way when you walk in your purpose, doing what He created you to do.

2 Tim 1:9 Who hath saved us, and called us with an holy calling, not according to our works, but according to his own purpose and grace, which was given us in Christ Jesus before the world began

1 *Prayer:* *Father, help me to have godly goals that line up with your Word and your will for my life.........................in Jesus' name, amen.*

Exercise: List three goals you have for your future.

4. _____

_____

_____

5. _____

_____

_____

6. _____

_____

_____

God can keep you on track

No one wants you to walk in your purpose more than God, for you are His product and His creation. As His product, you come with instructions and there's a manual that tells how you should operate. This manual is called the Bible. Fulfilling your purpose makes God look good and He likes that because it shows others that his product works and encourages others to read the manual. God also helps to keep us heading in the right direction. There are several ways that God can keep us focused on our purpose. Have you ever noticed that you can pray for some things for years and nothing happens? Then there are things you pray for and before you get off of your knees, it is done. This is one of the ways that God keeps us heading in the right direction. I have heard people say that you should be careful what you ask God for because He may give it to you, but I have found that our heavenly Father will not give us anything that is going to be detrimental to our purpose. Although I have, at times, gotten ahold of things that were not good for me, I can truly say that God did not give them to me. I took them on my own, which didn't work out so well for me.

Job 33:15-17 gives us an example of how God keeps us heading in the right direction.

Job 33:15-17 In a dream, in a vision of the night, when deep sleep falleth upon men, in slumberings upon the bed; 16 Then he openeth the ears of men, and sealeth their instruction, 17 that he may withdraw man from his purpose, and hide pride from man.

God will, at times, when we seem to be getting away from our purpose, give us a dream that will impresses us with warnings not to do something that we might be planning to do. How many times have you made an unwise decision and afterward said, "Something told me not to do that"? It happens all the time. Some children have dreams and fantasies about what they want to be when they grow up. That may be God pushing them toward their purpose. That is why adults should never tell a child that their goals and dreams are unattainable.

I must warn you that when God begins to reveals your purpose, Satan is going to want you to think that it is not true. He may even, as time goes on, want you to think that God has changed His mind about you. Don't believe it! God's purposes have not changed and His purpose for you has not changed.

2

Prayer: *Father, allow me to hear you in my dreams. Father, direct me in my dreams and show me the ways that I should go. Thank you. In the name of Jesus I pray.....................amen*

Exercise: List at least one dream that you have had that you think may have revealed your purpose.

What if

What if I have a bad dream? Is it from God?

Jer.23:28

7. _____

_____

_____

_____

_____

_____

_____

_____

God is a predictable God

As a child, I grew up in church and, because of incorrect teaching, I was left with a lot of preconceived notions about God. I had been taught that God is a mystery and that He is unpredictable. "You never know what God is going to do," they would say. But after studying the Bible for myself, I have come to the conclusion that God *is* predictable, and we can know what He is going to do. Let's be real. Could you really trust someone if you didn't know what they were going to do from one minute to the next? God is very predictable if you continue to seek Him. God is going to do exactly what His Word says because He cannot lie.

Num. 23:19 *God is not a man that he should lie; neither the son of man that he should repent: hath he said, and shall he not do it? Or hath he spoken, and shall he not make it good?*

When I got this revelation it changed my life. I began to ask God to teach me how to align my life with His Word, not so much for the present but for the future. As God begins to work His Word in our lives, we can align ourselves on the right side of the Word, which allows us to somewhat predict our future. Now that's exciting! Let's look at more scriptures that teach this truth:

Mal 3:6 *for I am the Lord, I change not; therefore, ye sons of Jacob are not consumed.*

Heb. 13:8 *Jesus Christ the same yesterday, and today, and forever.*

Understanding that God is going to do what He has said He would do can help us in every area of our lives. When we understand what God is going to do, then we know what we should do. Knowing what God wants and understanding what God expects of us lets us know how to live our lives and what to look forward to.

Prayer: Lord help me and show me how to align my life with your Word. I have a desire to please you in everything that I do. Teach me, Father, and show me the way....................................... in Jesus' name I pray, amen.

3

Exercise: What changes can you make in your life that will align you with what God is doing in your life now or you feel He is going to do?

8. _____

_____

_____

9. _____

_____

_____

10. _____

_____

_____

11. _____

_____

_____

Tyrone Johnson

Prayer: *Father, give me insight into your will for my life. In Jesus' name I pray..…......... amen*

Exercise: List on line 12 below how lines 4, 5, 6 from page 8 (Tab 1) compare to line 7 from page 12 (Tab 2).

12. _____

_____

_____

_____

_____

_____

_____

_____

_____

_____

Prayer: *Father, show me what you would have me to see that is in my heart. I understand that what is in my heart is what you have allowed the Holy Spirit to place there. In Jesus' name I pray...amen*

Exercise: Do you see any similarities on line 8, 9, 10, and 11 from page 15 (Tab 3) to line 7 from page 12 (Tab 2)? If yes, note below on line 13.

13. _____

_____

_____

_____

_____

_____

_____

_____

_____

_____

Chapter II

Can We Really Identify Our God-given Purpose?

Follow your heart?

The word *heart* in Hebrew is pronounced (***leb***) *also used (figuratively) very widely for the feelings, the will and even the intellect; likewise, for the center of anything.* The Greek word for heart is (***kardia***) and that is where we get our English word ***carotid*** (the name of the artery that goes to the heart*). It has basically the same meaning as the Hebrew definition: *the middle or central or inmost part of anything.* The question is, should we always follow our heart? The

> *What if*
>
> *What if I want to check my heart to see if it is in the right place?*
>
> *Matt. 6:21*

answer to that question will depend on whom you ask. After extensive research, I have concluded that most people think that following your heart is a good idea, which explains why most people are living a troubled life. On the other hand, the way that God deals with us or speaks to us is primarily in our hearts, so what are we to do? Let's go to the Bible and see what the Creator said about following your heart.

Jer 17:5-10 Thus saith the Lord; Cursed be the man that trusteth in man, and maketh flesh his arm, and whose heart departeth from the Lord. 6 For he shall be like the heath in the desert, and shall not see when good cometh; but shall inhabit the parched places in the wilderness, in a salt land and not inhabited. 7 Blessed is the man that trusteth in the Lord, and whose hope the Lord is. 8 For he shall be as a tree planted by the waters, and that spreadeth out her roots by the river, and shall not see when heat cometh, but her leaf shall be green; and shall not be careful in the year of drought, neither shall cease from yielding fruit. 9 The heart is deceitful above all things, and desperately wicked: who can know it? 10 I the Lord search the heart, I try the reins, even to give every man according to his ways, and according to the fruit of his doings.

The Lord said that if we depart from Him and put our trust in man, we place ourselves under a curse, and we know that won't end well for us. Verse 6 said we will be like the heath. *The Message* translation said it like this:

Jer 17:6 He's like a tumbleweed on the prairie, out of touch with the good earth. He lives rootless and aimless in a land where nothing grows.

So here we see that allowing our heart to depart from God is definitely not a good idea. Verses 7 and 8 gives us the benefits of trusting God, which is always a good thing. But the scary part of this text is verse 9: *the heart is deceitful above all things, and desperately wicked: who can know it?*

Can you imagine following your own heart and being deceived by it? Being self-deceived is the easiest thing to do. We expect other people to lie to us, so we don't listen too much to them, but we don't think we'd lie to ourselves. There is no deception like self-deception.

Tyrone Johnson

Prayer: *Father, create in me a clean heart, O God; and renew a right spirit within me........in the name of Jesus, I pray, amen.*

Exercise: Note at least one time you followed your heart and it took you the wrong way.

14. _____

_____

_____

_____

_____

_____

_____

_____

_____

_____

_____

We need a heart checkup

Before you can begin searching your heart for your purpose, you must make sure that your heart is right with God. In other words, we need a heart checkup. For salvation to work, there must be an honest relationship between the heart and the mouth. Note:

Rom 10:9-10 That if thou shalt confess with thy mouth the Lord Jesus, and shalt believe in thine heart that God hath raised him from the dead, thou shalt be saved.10 For with the heart man believeth unto righteousness; and with the mouth confession is made unto salvation.

We must believe in our heart what we are saying with our mouth, which is that Jesus is alive and that He is Lord over our lives. *Lord* in this instance means *"controller, owner."* One might wonder, "What difference does it make whether I say it or not, as long as I believe in my heart?" There are two very important things that confession does. It tells others what we believe in our hearts, which makes a good witness for Jesus. It also helps make me accountable to what I have just confessed.

Prayer: *Lord, let the words of my mouth, and the meditation of my heart be acceptable in thy sight, O Lord, my strength, and my redeemer .... In Jesus' name, I pray, amen.*

Exercise: List on line 15 at least one thing that you said you would do and when the time came you didn't want to do it, but you did it anyway because you had already confessed that you would.

15. _____

_____

_____

_____

_____

_____

_____

_____

Notice what Jesus teaches in Matt. 15:18. He said the mouth simply reveals what is already in the heart.

Matt 15:18 But those things which proceed out of the mouth come forth from the heart; and they defile the man.

What a great lesson. "If the heart is not right then the man will not be right." This is why it is so important that we allow God to work with our hearts before we search our hearts for purpose. In fact, before we search our hearts for *anything*, we need a heart checkup. We will not be able to change our hearts by changing what we say. Only God can change a man's heart. We see this same principle taught again in Matt. 12: 34-35.

Matt 12:34-35 O generation of vipers, how can ye, being evil, speak good things? for out of the abundance of the heart the mouth speaketh.35 A good man out of the good treasure of the heart bringeth forth good things: and an evil man out of the evil treasure bringeth forth evil things.

Prayer: *Father, you said that if I delight in you then you would place desires in my heart Father, help me to take delight in you so that my heart will only desire your will for my life..................................... In Jesus' name I pray, amen*

4 **Exercise: Note at least one heart desire that you had <u>before</u> you accepted Christ.**

16. _____

_____

_____

_____

Exercise: Note at least one heart desire that you had <u>after</u> you accepted Christ.

17. _____

_____

_____

_____

Understanding the will of the Lord

It is very important that we understand the will of the Lord, not only in general but for our personal lives. We need to know what God intended for us in this life so we will know how to plan for it. Suppose you want to be a doctor and you go to college for four years and get your degree and then go another four years to medical school, followed by two years of internship. You finish all that only to find out that God wanted you to be a lawyer. Now you have to start all over again.

When Paul speaks to the Ephesians about the will of the Lord, he calls them dead and says that they were asleep, not because they were not breathing but because they were not walking in the will of the Lord. What a radical concept to compare being dead with being out of the will of God. Paul tells them that if they would get up and look, Christ would show them the way. He also tells them that when

> *What If*
>
> *What if I plan something and I know it is what God wants, but it is just not happening*
>
> *Eccl. 3:1*

Christ shows them, they shouldn't be fools and ignore the Lord's will, but walk in it. Paul uses the phrase *"days are evil,"* meaning you don't have time to waste.

Eph 5:14-17 *Wherefore he saith, Awake thou that sleepest, and arise from the dead, and Christ shall give thee light.15 See then that ye walk circumspectly, not as fools, but as wise,16 Redeeming the time, because the days are evil.17 Wherefore be ye not unwise, but understanding what the will of the Lord is.*

Too often we make the mistake of not planning to succeed. Some of us may not make a plan at all. We may not understand that by not making a plan, we are actually planning to fail. Contrary to popular belief, God does not plan our lives for us. We must make our own plan and our plan must be in line with God's will for us. Then and only then will God help us follow it. God knows what is going on in our lives and He knows what is going to happen in our lives because of his sovereignty, but He is not the reason we make bad decisions. Prov. 16:9 said man makes the plan but God directs the steps.

Prov 16:9 *A man's heart deviseth his way: but the Lord directeth his steps*

Tyrone Johnson

Prayer: *Lord, order my steps in thy word: and let not any iniquity have dominion over me................... In the name of Jesus I pray, amen*

Exercise: List at least one time in your life that you planned something big or small and did it.

18. _____

_____

_____

_____

_____

_____

_____

_____

_____

_____

_____

This is an example of you making a plan in your heart and God directing your steps to bring it to pass.

What do I really want?

It might surprise you to learn that God is concerned about what you want. Yes, God has a purpose for your life, but God is no dummy. He knows that if you enjoy something, you will do a better job at it. One might ask the question, "Suppose God has one purpose for me and I want to do something else?" That is a good question and, believe me, it happens all the time. When God wants one thing and we want another, there is a process that God will allow us to go through. This process is the reason most people do not start to truly walk in their purpose until late in their lives. Let's look at the process in Rom. 12:1-2.

Rom 12:1-2 I beseech you therefore, brethren, by the mercies of God, that ye present your bodies a living sacrifice, holy, acceptable unto God, which is your reasonable service. 2 And be not conformed to this world: but be ye transformed by the renewing of your mind, that ye may prove what is that good, and acceptable, and perfect, will of God.

In Rom. chapter 11, Paul has just spoken about the mercies of God toward us, which should cause us to appreciate and love God. When we love someone, we want to please them. Paul then starts chapter 12 by telling us how we should respond to God's mercy, which is with sacrifice or the willingness to change. Paul also uses the word *service*, which means *helpful activity*, so we know that we should be doing something. In Rom.12:2, Paul said we should be doing God's will, but he uses the word *"prove"* which is pronounced *"dokimazo"* and comes from the word *"dokimos,"* which means *"approve."* The process involves continuing to renew your mind until you begin to think like God. When you think like God, you will see things the same way God sees them, and God's will become your will. Then you will approve of God's will for your life.

Exercise: Review the difference on line 16 and line 17 from page 26 (Tab 4). The two desires are different because one

was made from a heart that did not know God and the other was made from a heart that knew God.

We find this same principle at work in Ps. 37:4.

Ps 37:4 Delight thyself also in the Lord; and he shall give thee the desires of thine heart.

The word delight in Ps. 37:4 is *"anag"* which means *"to be soft or pliable, able to bend, fold, or twist easily."* What God is telling us is that if we are soft toward Him and willing to allow Him to influence us, then He will place desires in our heart that He wants us to pursue. Here is how this works: if you are delighting yourself in the Lord, and God wants to give you a new car, you may not even be thinking about a new car, but God will place an urgent desire in your heart for a new car and then give you a new car.

Exercise: List below on line 19 at least one time in your life when you were seeking God and all of a sudden you had a desire for something. You didn't understand where that desire came from but you wanted it and went after it and God gave it to you.

19. _____

_____

_____

_____

_____

_____

_____

_____

_____

_____

This is an example of God placing a desire in your heart and then bringing it to pass.

Prayer: *Lord, I shall not be afraid of evil tidings, because my heart is fixed, trusting in you........................ In the name of Jesus, I pray, amen.*

Exercise: List five heart desires that you have now as a believer.

19. _____

_____

_____

20 _____

_____

_____

21 _____

_____

_____

22 _____

_____

_____

Tyrone Johnson

23 _____

_____

_____

24 _____

_____

_____

Chapter III

How Does God Say My Life Should be Lived?

In the previous chapters, we looked at a general overview of what scripture has to say about man's makeup as a whole and how man was created to function. In this chapter, we are going to focus on some specifics about how God said we should live our lives. But first we must answer the question of whether or not God has the right or authority to tell us how to live our lives. If you have accepted Jesus as savior and Lord of your life, then clearly, God has the right and authority to tell you how to live your life. The word Lord simply means *"owner"* so if He is your Lord than He is your owner and as the owner He has the right and authority to tell you what to do and what not to do. What might not be as clear is that, if you are not saved, He is *still* LORD *"owner."* Whether you accept it or not, God still has the right and authority over the unsaved person simply because He created them. For the purpose of clarity, we will break our life into three parts: our work life, our home life, and our social life. To truly walk in our purpose, we must allow God to intervene in every area of our life: at work, at play, and at home.

My life at work will consist of:

a) My relationships at work or the lack thereof.

b) How should I behave at work?

c) What desires should I have for my work life?

d) Do I feel that my work is the will of the Lord?

My life at home will consist of:

a) My relationships with my family or the lack thereof.

What if

What if I have a desire to succeed but at the same time I am afraid to succeed?

Matt. 28:18-20

b) What should I expect from my family and what should they expect from me?

c) What desires should I have for my home life now and in the future?

d) Does the will of the Lord have free range in my home?

My social life will consist of:

a) The relationships that I have socially.

b) My life at church and my relationships there.

c) My overall social life.

d) What desires do I have for my social life now and in the future?

e) Would God approve of all of my social activities?

If you have worked through the previous excises being prayerful and honest with yourself, you may have found that your thinking and God's thinking are about the same. If you found that what God said and what you think are not the same, that is ok for now. You are about to learn what the scripture means when it said in Isa 1:18 *"Come now, and let us reason together…."* You must keep in mind that God needs you to succeed. The Bible says that when men see your good work, they will glorify your Father in heaven. When you succeed, you make God look good, so God will make sure you are on the right track if that is truly your heart's desire.

What does God say about my work life?

Before we get into what God said about our life at work, we must understand that God does not make rich people or poor people. God makes people. God does not even command us to stay away from poverty. Only a little over 7.5 percent of the Bible talks about poverty. It is as if it is of little concern to God; He loves us just the same if we are rich or poor, and He can use us whether we are rich or poor. It simply isn't that big of a deal to God. The scriptures do warn against seeking after earthly riches and, if we find ourselves with earthly riches, the scriptures teach us how to handle them in a way that will glorify God.

I am a true believer that God wants us to have all the earthly riches that we can handle. Otherwise, why would the Bible speak about riches and poverty? I also believe that God leaves it up to us to choose. When we don't choose, this is still a choice. We make a choice by choosing not to make a choice.

What If

What if I want to be rich and I still want to walk in God's will?

I Tim. 6:17-19

We associate riches and poverty with our work life because most of us relate our work to how much riches we have. That is exactly the type of thinking that I want to change with this workbook. There are many scriptures that speak about this, but I have chosen just a few. First, we will look at what causes poverty, and then we will look at how we stay away from poverty. Last, we will look at how God wants us to relate to our employer.

Tyrone Johnson

What causes poverty?

Prov 24:30-34 *I went by the field of the slothful, and by the vineyard of the man void of understanding; 31 And, lo, it was all grown over with thorns, and nettles had covered the face thereof, and the stone wall thereof was broken down. 32 Then I saw, and considered it well: I looked upon it, and received instruction. 33 Yet a little sleep, a little slumber, a little folding of the hands to sleep: 34 So shall thy poverty come as one that travelleth; and thy want as an armed man.*

Prov. 24:30-34 simply states if I don't do anything, poverty will come. This principle fascinated me because I have always been taught to just wait on the Lord. But waiting on the Lord doesn't mean that I become lazy. If you think that way, you are void of understanding. This principle works just like the command that God gave us to train up a child. If we don't train our children to do the right thing, they will automatically do the wrong thing. Do you teach your child to lie, steal, or be mean to other children? Of course not. This principle is true in every area of our lives, because we were

42

all born in sin. If not corrected, we will just gravitate toward the wrong things. That is the way poverty works. If we don't do anything to keep it away, it just shows up at our door and invites itself in and doesn't leave until we make it leave.

Prov. 24:34 said poverty comes as one that *"travelleth."* This indicates that poverty comes walking, which means it doesn't happen overnight. When poverty shows up in our lives, it will always bring *want*, and want will be like an armed man—it will rob you of what little you do have. I believe that the enemy uses poverty to get us out of God's will, and he is having some success at it. But we can change that through good Bible teaching.

Prayer: *Father, remove far from me vanity and lies. Give me neither poverty nor riches. Feed me with food convenient for me, lest I be full and deny thee and say, Who is the Lord? or lest I be poor and steal and take the name of my God in vain.................in Jesus' name I pray, amen.*

Exercise: List at least one time that you made an ungodly decision for monetary gain.

25. _____

_____

_____

_____

_____

_____

_____

_____

_____

_____

Your work and your job

There is a big difference between your work and your job. Our goal should be that our work and our job be the same, but too often that is not the case. Your job is what your employer pays you to do, but your work is what God created you to do. God told man in Gen. 2:15 to dress the garden. Some of the modern translations translated the Hebrew word *"aabdaah"* as work instead of dress, but the meaning is basically the same: to *"arrange."* God gave man the task of managing the garden. Man didn't have to make the garden grow; it would do that on its own. Man just had to arrange it when it grew.

Gen 2:5...for the Lord God had not caused it to rain upon the earth, and there was not a man to till the ground.

Notice God withheld the rain so that the garden would not grow until He created man to manage the garden. God does the same thing in our lives. He will withhold certain things from us until we learn how to manage them.

Let's look at another scripture that talks about the difference between our work and our job.

***Eccl 11:6** In the morning sow thy seed, and in the evening withhold not thine hand: for thou knowest not whether shall prosper, either this or that, or whether they both shall be alike good.*

To sow your seed in the morning means go to your job and do what you are being paid to do. That is sowing seed, and when you get paid, that is your harvest. Note that in the evening you don't withhold your hand. Rather, in the evening, you work on what God created you for. "*...for thou knowest not whether shall prosper, either this or that, or whether they both shall be alike good.*"

Anyone can be fired from their job, but you can never be fired from your work. Your work is tied in with your gift from God, and if you leave, your gift goes with you. Even though God wants you to focus on maturing your gift, He doesn't want you to neglect your job. God teaches us in 1Thess 4:11-12 how to conduct ourselves on our job.

1 Thess 4:11-12 And that ye study to be quiet, and to do your own business, and to work with your own hands, as we commanded you; 12 That ye may walk honestly toward them that are without, and that ye may have lack of nothing.

Verse 11 is saying mind your business and do your job. Verse 12 tells us that the unsaved people are watching, and God wants us to appear honest to the unsaved, which will glorify God. The other benefit is that you get a paycheck and you use it to meet your needs so you lack nothing.

Prayer: *Father teach me to let my light shine before men, that they may see my good works and glorify you in heaven.................... In Jesus' name I pray, amen.*

Exercise: List below at least three things that you would like to change about yourself relating to your job.

5

26. _____

_____

_____

_____

27. _____

_____

_____

_____

28. _____

_____

_____

_____

How do I relate to my employer?

Everything that we do in this earth will in some way affect our relationship with others. The types of relationships that we form are critical to our purpose in the earth, so we should seek to form good and proper relationships. The Bible gives us detailed instructions about our relationship with our employer. For example, if your employer hasn't accepted Christ into their life, that doesn't mean you shouldn't enjoy working for them. This will just give you more opportunity to glorify God in their presence. Eph. 6:5-9 tells us how to relate to our employer even if they are not saved.

Eph 6:5-9 Servants, be obedient to them that are your masters according to the flesh, with fear and trembling, in singleness of your heart, as unto Christ; 6 Not with eyeservice, as menpleasers; but as the servants of Christ, doing the will of God from the heart; 7 With good will doing service, as to the Lord, and not to men: 8 Knowing that whatsoever good thing any man doeth, the same shall he receive of the Lord, whether he be bond or free. 9 And, ye masters, do the same things unto them, forbearing threatening: knowing that your Master also is in heaven; neither is there respect of persons with him.

Your employer is buying a certain amount of your time for an agreed-on designated purpose, so if you do not deliver, you are stealing.

Note what it says in verse 5 .... *be obedient.... according to the flesh, with fear and trembling, in singleness of your heart, as unto Christ*

We honor Christ when we do the right things. We are not to do a good job only when the boss is looking or to look good to fellow workers,

"but as the servants of Christ, doing the will of God from the heart."

A careful study of this text reveals that, even if you are working for an unbeliever, you are still working for God. As a child of God, we must remember that we represent God in everything that we do.

My life at home

The average American spends about 45 percent of their time at home. If you are not pleased with how things are going at home, then you spend almost half of your time being unhappy. Everyone has things in their life that they would like to improve, but how do we do it? After all, we can only change ourselves.

Fortunately, changing yourself will cause your whole household to change. This is called "the ripple effect." You just need to know what you want it to change into. Note Prov. 14:1:

Prov 14:1 *Every wise woman buildeth her house: but the foolish plucketh it down with her hands.*

The word build means to *"make, repair, set up."* The way this verb is used here—*"buildeth"*—means that this is a continued action. The verse is telling us that a wise woman will continually make her house, she will continually repair her house, and she will continually set up her house. The ripple effect means that she can also tear down her house by what she does, but only a foolish woman would do so. Now let's look at what God said about our individual relationships in the home.

Your life with your spouse

As you begin to identify your God-given purpose, you might be surprised to find what a huge part your spouse plays in your purpose. Besides God, your spouse is the most important person in your life. When you begin to walk in your calling, you will find that the mate that God has given you will fit perfectly with what God has called you to do. That is part of what Gen. 2:24 means when it says "the two shall become one."

According to a new Office Pulse survey taken in early 2017, a whopping 70 percent of business professionals currently work with their spouse at the office or have in the past. That's up from the 65 percent in 2010 and 32 percent in 2006. It appears that the secular community is beginning to act out

Gen.2:24: *Therefore shall a man leave his father and his mother, and shall cleave unto his wife…*

In Eph. 5:22, God commands the wife to submit herself to her husband, and in Eph. 5:23 God commands the husband to love his wife. It is worded this way because submission is easier for

> **What If**
>
> What if I am saved and my spouse is not, will I still be able to walk in my purpose?
>
> I Cor. 7:19

men whereas love comes easier for women. A man must make a conscious effort to show love to his wife, but showing love to her husband may come more naturally to a woman. In the same way, a man may find it effortless to submit to his wife while women struggle with submission. Notice that God always requires us to go down the narrow road.

Eph 5:22-23 Wives, submit yourselves unto your own husbands, as unto the Lord.23 For the husband is the head of the wife, even as Christ is the head of the church: and he is the saviour of the body.

Eph 5:25 *Husbands, love your wives, even as Christ also loved the church, and gave himself for it.*

Make sure that your relationship with your spouse is always in good standing so that your prayers will not be hindered. Remember that God sees the two as one and as one you should go before God together. As you seek your purpose, you must be prayerful, and if your prayers are hindered, it will be very difficult, if not impossible, to hear from God.

1 Peter 3:7 commands us to dwell together according to knowledge. This means we need to know our spouse and refrain from doing things that we know they don't like.

1 Peter 3:7 *Likewise, ye husbands, dwell with them according to knowledge, giving honour unto the wife, as unto the weaker vessel, and as being heirs together of the grace of life; that your prayers be not hindered.*

Prayer: *Father help me to dwell with my spouse according to knowledge, giving them honour so that my prayers be not hindered .... in Jesus' name I pray, amen.*

Exercise: List at least three things below that you would like to change about your relationship with your spouse.

29. _____

_____

_____

_____

30. _____

_____

_____

_____

31. _____

_____

_____

_____

6

Tyrone Johnson

My life with my children

Your earthly purpose is going to encompass every area of your life, including your children. Have you ever noticed that most children of preachers become preachers? My father was a preacher and all thru the unsaved part of my life, somehow I knew I was going to be a preacher. I wasn't in any hurry to get started, though. I was forty years old before I accepted Christ into my life and forty-two before I started preaching. I regret my decision to wait to get started until so late in my life every day.

Statistics show that about 70 percent of children will follow in their parents' footsteps. With stats like that, we parents cannot afford to get it wrong. The parent-child relationship is probably the most difficult relationship in the home to maintain because it is always changing. Unlike the spouse relationship, which is simply "until death do you part," there will come a time in the parent-child relationship where the man leaves his father and mother and cleaves to his wife. Another difference is that the parent-child relationship in not usually a voluntary one. We don't usually get to pick who our children are, we simply work with what God gives us.

We must remember that our children are a gift from God. He gives them to us for a certain amount of time and we shouldn't try to hold on to them. At the right time, we must let them go. The Bible has a lot to say about parent-child relationships. Let's just look at a few scriptures.

Eph 6:1-3 Children, obey your parents in the Lord: for this is right.2 Honour thy father and mother; (which is the first commandment with promise ;)3 That it may be well with thee, and thou mayest live long on the earth.

Notice how God does not overstep the parents' authority. God allows the parent to be the middleman between God and the child as long as the parent is *in the Lord*. God knows that as long as the parents are in the Lord, they will only give the child godly instructions, which He commands the child to obey. God rewards our children with long life simply for obeying their parents. Isn't that a great deal?

Prov 22:6 *Train up a child in the way he should go: and when he is old, he will not depart from it.*

God commands us to train up our children in the way that they should go, which is the Lord's way, so that when our children are old, they will not depart from it. Note that the word *it* is the training that they will not depart from. Don't confuse the training with the parent. Our children may depart from us, but they won't depart from the training. They will always remember what their parents have taught them, whether they live it out in their lives or not.

Ps 127:3-5 *Lo, children are an heritage of the Lord: and the fruit of the womb is his reward. 4 As arrows are in the hand of a mighty man; so are children of the youth. 5 Happy is the man that hath his quiver full of them: they shall not be ashamed, but they shall speak with the enemies in the gate.*

Prayer: *Father help me to bring up my children in the nurture and admonition of the Lord......................in Jesus' name I pray, amen.*

Exercise: List at least two things below that you would like to change about your relationship with your children.

32. _____

_____

_____

_____

_____

33. _____

_____

_____

_____

_____

7

Tyrone Johnson

My social life

A believer's social life should encompass everything that they do, but for the purpose of clarity, let's define social life as outside of work or home. Our social life will be about one third of our lives, and it will entail our interpersonal relationships with people within our immediate surroundings or the general public. As a Christian, there is nothing more satisfying than getting together with other believers in fellowship. In fact, God has ordained and blessed our fellowship with each other. Note:

Ps 133:1-3 Behold, how good and how pleasant it is for brethren to dwell together in unity! 2 It is like the precious ointment upon the head, that ran down upon the beard, even Aaron's beard: that went down to the skirts of his garments; 3 As the dew of Hermon, and as the dew that descended upon the mountains of Zion: for there the Lord commanded the blessing, even life for evermore.

Let's look at some other scriptures that speak about how we should relate to other believers:

Matt 18:15-17 Moreover if thy brother shall trespass against thee, go and tell him his fault between thee and him alone: if he shall hear thee, thou hast gained thy brother.16 But if he will not hear thee, then take with thee one or two more, that in the mouth of two or three witnesses every word may be established. 17 And if he shall neglect to hear them, tell it unto the church: but if he neglect to hear the church, let him be unto thee as an heathen man and a publican.

Amos 3:3 Can two walk together, except they be agreed?

We can see from these scriptures that God wants us to fellowship and get alone with each other. After all, we are one big family of believers that belong to the Lord. We also know that it is impossible to live in this world and have no interactions with unbelievers, although some have tried it. Paul chastised the believers in Corinth for attempting the very same thing. Paul tells them that if they want to have no interactions with unbelievers, they will have to go out of this world.

__1 Cor 5:9-10__ I wrote unto you in an epistle not to company with fornicators:10 Yet not altogether with the fornicators of this world, or with the covetous, or extortioners, or with idolaters; for then must ye needs go out of the world

Since we will have to interact with unbelievers, it is important that we understand how to relate to them in a social setting. How we relate socially is critical because that is when we are relaxed and our guard is down, allowing the real us to shine through. The Bible teaches us that we are in the world but not of the world. While we are in the world, we must follow the same laws the world follows. We shop at the same stores that the world shops at and we go to the same restaurants that the world goes to. We will need good social skills in order to fulfill our God-given purpose in the world. In order for us the win people to Christ, we must be able to relate to them on a social level because it is not possible on a spiritual level. We must become what some would call a *"social butterfly."* In Matt. 10:16 we are commanded to be wise as *"serpents."* A serpent blends in with its surroundings, and you usually can't see them from a distance. Jesus blended in so well that when the Roman soldiers came to arrest him, they needed Judas to point him out. They could not recognize Him because He looked like everybody else, physically.

Matt 10:16 *Behold, I send you forth as sheep in the midst of wolves: be ye therefore wise as serpents, and harmless as doves.*

We have always been taught that as believers we should stand out, but a careful study of the Bible reveals that it speaks also about blending in. In order for us to influence the world for the kingdom of God, we must be able to become all things to all people. Paul said it like this:

Phil 4:11-12 *Not that I speak in respect of want: for I have learned, in whatsoever state I am, therewith to be content.12 I know both how to be abased, and I know how to abound: every where and in all things I am instructed both to be full and to be hungry, both to abound and to suffer need.*

Tyrone Johnson

Prayer: *Father, teach me to number my days, that we may apply my heart unto wisdom... in Jesus' name I pray, amen.*

Exercise: List at least three things below that you would like to change about yourself related to a social life.

34. _____

_____

_____

_____

8 **35.** _____

_____

_____

_____

36 _____

_____

_____

_____

CHAPTER IV

Time to Get Honest

Sometimes the hardest person to be honest with is yourself because we often think of ourselves in terms of how we want to be and not how we really are. It is so easy to look at what God said we should be and think that we are already that person, and therefore see no need for change. You may find it very helpful as you answer some of the tough questions in this chapter to speak to someone who knows you and who doesn't mind hurting your feelings, "in love," of course.

Hopefully, you have completed all of the previous exercises so that your thinking is on the right track. If your thinking is wrong than your conclusion will be wrong, so let's review.

In the introduction, we mentioned five things that we had to accept if we want to identify our purpose and they were:

1) *God had a purpose in mind when He created me,*

2) *My purpose is greater than I am,*

3) *God placed my purpose in me,*

4) *God wants me to know and fulfill my purpose,*

5) *Only I can forfeit my purpose.*

In chapter 1, we identified some common problems that people run into relating to the above five things. Then we identified some goals that we have for our life. We then took a brief look at how the goals we had lined up with God's Word. In chapter 2, we explored the danger in following our heart and looked at how our heart's desire may change at different stages of our life. In chapter 3, we looked at what God had to say about our life at work, at home, and at play.

We must be very prayerful as we move into this final section. Remember in chapter 2 when we talked about the dangers of following your heart? Following your heart can be a great thing, as long as you have a heart that is seeking God's will for your life. The only way to do that is through prayer. Most of the time, God speaks to you through your heart, but we must make sure that it is God that is speaking and not Satan or ourselves. God will often use His Word, the Bible, to speak to us, or to confirm what He has spoken in our hearts. I believe that the reason God uses His written Word is so that we won't get confused about who is speaking.

Tyrone Johnson

Prayer: *Father, order my steps in thy word and let not any iniquity have dominion over me..........................in the name of Jesus I pray, amen.*

Your Job or Work life

Exercise: Review your entries (Tab 5) on lines 26, 27, and 28 from page 48 and rewrite them so that they will be in line with what the Word of God said. If they don't need to be changed, just rewrite them on lines 37, 38, and 39 on page 70 (Tab9). Use the scriptures below to make sure they are in line with God's Word.

Prov 24:30-34 *I went by the field of the slothful, and by the vineyard of the man void of understanding;31 And, lo, it was all grown over with thorns, and nettles had covered the face thereof, and the stone wall thereof was broken down.32 Then I saw, and considered it well: I looked upon it, and received instruction.33 Yet a little sleep, a little slumber, a little folding of the hands to sleep:34 So shall thy poverty come as one that travelleth; and thy want as an armed man.*

Eccl 11:6 *In the morning sow thy seed, and in the evening withhold not thine hand: for thou knowest not whether shall prosper, either this or that, or whether they both shall be alike good.*

Eph 6:5-9 *Servants, be obedient to them that are your masters according to the flesh, with fear and trembling, in singleness of your heart, as unto Christ; 6 Not with eyeservice, as menpleasers; but as the servants of Christ, doing the will of God from the heart; 7 With good will doing service, as to the Lord, and not to men: 8 Knowing that whatsoever good thing any man doeth, the same shall he receive of the Lord, whether he be bond or free. 9 And, ye masters, do the same things unto them, forbearing threatening: knowing that your Master also is in heaven; neither is there respect of persons with him.*

37. _____

_____

_____

_____

_____

38. _____

_____

_____

_____

9 **39** _____

_____

_____

_____

_____

Prayer: *Father, you hast commanded us to keep thy precepts diligently. O that my ways were directed to keep thy statutes................................in the name of Jesus I pray, amen.*

Exercise: Review your entries on (Tab 9) lines 37, 38, and 39 from page 70 and combine them into one statement and write it on line 40 below (Tab 10).

40. _____

_____

_____

_____

_____

10

_____

_____

_____

_____

_____

Your home life

Exercise: Review your entries on lines (Tab 6) 29, 30, and 31 from page 55 and (Tab 7) lines 32 and 33 from page 59 then rewrite them so that they are in line with what the Word of God said. If they don't need to be changed, just rewrite them on lines 41, 42, 43, 44, and 45 on page 74 (Tab 11). Use the scriptures below to make sure they are in line with God's Word.

Prov 14:1 *Every wise woman buildeth her house: but the foolish plucketh it down with her hands.*

Eph 5:22-23 *Wives, submit yourselves unto your own husbands, as unto the Lord. 23 For the husband is the head of the wife, even as Christ is the head of the church: and he is the saviour of the body.*

Eph 5:25 *Husbands, love your wives, even as Christ also loved the church, and gave himself for it;*

1 Peter 3:7 Likewise, ye husbands, dwell with them according to knowledge, giving honour unto the wife, as unto the weaker vessel, and as being heirs together of the grace of life; that your prayers be not hindered.

Eph 6:1-3 Children, obey your parents in the Lord: for this is right.2 Honour thy father and mother; (which is the first commandment with promise;)3 That it may be well with thee, and thou mayest live long on the earth.

Prov 22:6 Train up a child in the way he should go: and when he is old, he will not depart from it.

Ps 127:3-5 Lo, children are an heritage of the Lord: and the fruit of the womb is his reward. 4 As arrows are in the hand of a mighty man; so are children of the youth. 5 Happy is the man that hath his quiver full of them: they shall not be ashamed, but they shall speak with the enemies in the gate.

Tyrone Johnson

41.

_____

_____

_____

42

_____

_____

_____

43.

_____

_____

_____

44.

_____

_____

_____

45

_____

_____

_____

11

Prayer: Father, your word have I hid in mine heart. Help me that I might not sin against thee...................in the name of Jesus I pray, amen

Exercise: **Review your entries (*Tab 11*) on lines 41, 42, 43, 44, and 45 *from pages 73* and combine them into one sentence on line 46 *below (Tab12).***

46. _____

_____

_____

_____

_____

_____

_____

_____

12

_____

_____

Prayer: *Father, help me to cleanse my way and take heed thereto according to thy word............in Jesus' name I pray, amen.*

Your social life

Exercise: Review your entries (Tab 8) on lines 34, 35, and 36 from page 64 then rewrite them that they are in line with what the Word of God said. If they don't need to be changed, just rewrite them on lines 47, 48, and 49 page 78 (Tab 13). Use the scriptures below to make sure they are in line with God's Word.

Ps 133:1-3 *Behold, how good and how pleasant it is for brethren to dwell together in unity! 2 It is like the precious ointment upon the head, that ran down upon the beard, even Aaron's beard: that went down to the skirts of his garments; 3 As the dew of Hermon, and as the dew that descended upon the mountains of Zion: for there the Lord commanded the blessing, even life for evermore.*

Matt 18:15-17 *Moreover if thy brother shall trespass against thee, go and tell him his fault between thee and him alone: if he* *shall hear thee, thou hast gained thy brother.16 But if he will not hear thee, then take with thee one or two more, that in the mouth of two or three witnesses every word may be established. 17 And if he shall neglect to hear them, tell it unto the church: but if he neglect to hear the church, let him be unto thee as an heathen man and a publican.*

Amos 3:3 Can two walk together, except they be agreed?

1 Cor 5:9-10 I wrote unto you in an epistle not to company with fornicators:10 Yet not altogether with the fornicators of this world, or with the covetous, or extortioners, or with idolaters; for then must ye needs go out of the world

Matt 10:16 Behold, I send you forth as sheep in the midst of wolves: be ye therefore wise as serpents, and harmless as doves.

Phil 4:11-12 Not that I speak in respect of want: for I have learned, in whatsoever state I am, therewith to be content.12 I know both how to be abased, and I know how to abound: every where and in all things I am instructed both to be full and to be hungry, both to abound and to suffer need.

47. _____

_____

_____

_____

_____

48. _____

_____

_____

_____

_____

49 _____

_____

_____

_____

_____

13

Prayer: *Father, I will delight myself in thy statutes. Help me not forget thy word...in the name of Jesus I pray, amen.*

Exercise: Review entries (*Tab 13*) on lines 47, 48, and 49, *from page 77* and combine them into one sentence and write in on line 50 *below (Tab 14).*

50. _____

_____

_____

_____

_____

_____

_____

_____

_____

14

My kingdom assignment

Being very prayerful, we can now look into our hearts and see what God has placed there, thereby understanding God's purpose for us. As we have made a list of the desires of our hearts and our desires are in line with the Word of God, it is time for us to understand our kingdom assignment.

Being prayerful, study your statements (*Tab 10)* on line 40 (page 71), (Tab 12) line 46 (page 75), and (Tab 14) line 50 (page 79). These three statements, which represent your work life, your home life, and your social life, also show the desires of your heart, which are in line with God's Word. While meditating on these statements, carefully rewrite them in one statement in a way that will reflect all three of them. After combining your three statements into one, write it on line 51 on page 81

Prayer: Father, help me to incline my ear unto wisdom and apply my heart to understanding; I know that you desire truth in the inward parts and in the hidden you shalt make me to know wisdom. So, Father, teach me to number my days, that we may apply my heart unto wisdom .... in Jesus' name I pray, amen.

51. _____

_____

This final statement shows your heart's desires and, as they are in line with God's Word, we must assume they were placed there by God. Please notice that your desires will change as your relationship with God grows, so it would be a good idea to repeat this workbook periodically. The statement on line 51, which represents your kingdom assignment, may not be precise but, assuming you completed all of the excises and followed the directions, it is very close and it certainly points you in the right direction.

Now that you are aware of your purpose, it could feel like your life has just begun. Knowing your purpose makes almost everything in your life make sense and it not only shows you what you should be doing but, more importantly, it shows you what you shouldn't be doing. Continue to be prayerful and seek God, as I will also be praying for you. May God bless you.

Father I pray a special blessing on everyone that completed this workbook. I that their purpose that their purpose will begin to manifest in their life. I pray that the enemy will get no victory, as that seek your will. I pray that you keep us heading in the right direction, as we fulfil your purposes in the earth. Teach us how to walk in your will. Father help us to understand that we will never know your will for our lives if we don't know you, give us a heart after your heart and those that have not accepted you as their savior give them a mind to want to know you, in the name of Jesus I pray amen

Printed in the United States
By Bookmasters